ROLL WITH ME

Towards a happier, more joyful and successful life.

JOHN C. KIRCHNER

E xulon
LITE

Dedication page

I dedicate this book to my father, John R Kirchner a.k.a. Kahuna.

Thanks to my father always being there for me and inspiring me, I was given the strength and the knowledge to be able to overcome any obstacle in my way. I would always tell my father before his passing that he will never die. He will live for eternity because I will share and pass on to others all that he has taught me in life. His spirit and his legacy will continue to live on forever. I pray these words that I share with you in this book will make as much of a positive impact in your life as they have in mine.

Acknowledgment page

First and foremost I thank the Lord above for giving me the words to use to inspire others.

A great bit of thanks also goes to Errica Jamil for helping motivate me to write this book. Thank you.

Table of Contents

Have you ever experienced a horrific car accident where the car rolled over and over and flipped end over end? You heard the metal crunching around you and the glass shatter right before your eyes. Every time the car rolled, you felt your head crash into the ground. Now picture yourself inside that car.

That is where I was twenty-eight years ago. Immediately following that accident, which almost took my life, I spent four-and-a-half months in the hospital. When I left, I was a quadriplegic, paralyzed from the neck down and sitting in a wheelchair for the rest of my life. I was told all the things I couldn't do anymore and would never be able to do again.

Being an active seventeen-year-old with a zest for living, it was not something I wanted to hear, nor was it something I would accept. I faced a lot of obstacles in my life, and I still continue to this day. However, over the past twenty-eight years, I have developed, applied, and perfected these principles in my life. They have enabled me to do more than many thought possible: it is helped me overcome obstacles; it has helped me deal with the ups and downs in life.

We all face challenges in life, and I know everyone is different; however, the tools we need to overcome, to break through, to be empowered, to find success, and to be joyful are always the same.

Do you have an obstacle that you want to overcome? Do you feel as if there is something dragging you down and holding you back from achieving your goals? Are you looking for a happier and more joyful life? These questions and more were ones that floated around in my head, and my answer was always the same: yes, and I will find a solution for all of them and I will be victorious. Roll with me and let me share with you what has made so many positive changes in my life.

"I Want Change"

Fundamental Principle #1:

Make a conscious decision that you want change in your life.

In order to live a happier, more joyful and successful life, you have to say to yourself, "I want change; I want to do something different with my life." I can't tell you how many times I have heard somebody say, "Things aren't going well for me; I hate my job; I can't ever catch a break; I'm always fighting with my kids or fighting with my spouse."

The list goes on and on, and I would ask them, "What are you doing to change all of that?"

More times than not, I heard the response, "Nothing."

Now, I will admit, for years and years after my accident I didn't do anything constructive. Sure, I hung out with friends, I did some traveling, and I was active, but as far as doing anything to better anyone else's life—let alone my own—I figuratively and literally sat on my butt. It wasn't until I was twenty-nine when I decided to make a profound change in my life, and for me, that was to quit drinking. I knew that was a huge obstacle in my way of achieving any dreams or goals I had in my life. I'll never forget the night I decided to quit drinking. I was in bed, trying to come up with a pros and cons list for drinking and I realized quickly there was nothing in the pros column, but when it came to the cons, that thing started to look like a laundry list. All the people I hurt, all the relationships I ruined, all the times I would wake up the next morning and have to apologize for my behavior the previous night—and then I looked in the corner of my room and saw my wheelchair. I realized partially the reason why I am in this chair is because of my drinking.

Right then, I swore I would never let something that took so much away from me control my life. That is when I decided I needed to make a change and I did that night. I swore off alcohol and prayed to the Lord that He would remove any desire to drink and because I serve a gracious and wonderful God, He did. A lot of my friends and even some of my family thought there was no way I would be able to do it and quite frankly, I didn't blame them. It was bad for the past ten years. However, after seeing me go week after week, then month after month without having a sip of alcohol, they changed their tune. I also noticed I stopped hanging out with a lot of my friends who still drank. I went down a different path—a better path for me—and I loved it. I saw life with a whole new perspective. I realized there's a whole lot more I could and should be doing, and before long, I had new friendships, new relationships, and doors of opportunity opened right before my eyes. Life began to change and it was definitely for the better and it all started that one night when I proclaimed I wanted change and I did it.

So if you are ready to start this journey of living a happier, more joyful, and successful life, the first thing you must do is discover what it is you feel holds you back. What is it that you want to change? The second thing is to write down *how* that change will make a difference in your life and the lives around you. Put that somewhere where you will see it everyday. Maybe your mirror in the bathroom. Read it everyday and soon, it will be imbedded in your brain. The third thing is to then proclaim out loud, "I am going to change now!" The fourth thing is to understand it will not happen overnight, but it *will* happen! You can't move a mountain in one day, but if you move a little each day, soon you won't see that mountain. Last, but definitely not least, trust in the Lord that He will give you the strength you need to change. He said if we do our best, He will take care of the rest and He always does.

"Putting It Into Perspective"

Fundamental Principle #2:

P ut things into perspective. Realize things are probably not as bad as you think.

Over the past twenty-seven years, I have come to realize pain is pain. It doesn't matter if you're in a wheelchair, you lost your job, you're going through a bad divorce, or any number of things. The bottom line is: sometimes in your life, you will experience pain. How we handle that pain though will make all the difference in the world.

When I was in the hospital recovering from my near-fatal car accident, I met a lot of other people who also faced similar challenges. Many of them were paralyzed from the waist down or had limited mobility in their arms, whereas I was paralyzed from the neck down. I thought to myself, *life must not be that bad for them*. Sure, they had some paralysis, but I thought they could still use their arms so they couldn't possibly be in the same amount of pain as me.

Boy, was I wrong.

I realized you could only associate with as much as you have experienced. So no matter their loss, it was as painful to them as my loss was to me. That is when it occurred to me that pain is pain, no matter what. However, I still thought being paralyzed from the neck down was as bad as it could possibly be. I believed that all the way up until something happened that completely changed how I viewed my situation.

I was in bed one night when all of a sudden, I heard the most heart-wrenching scream. I asked one of the nurses, "What is going on?" She told me they had brought in a fireman and while fighting the fire, a beam fell from the ceiling and crashed down on his neck, pinning him to the floor. Not only did he have a broken neck, but he also suffered third-degree burns over ninety percent of his body. I couldn't believe it. My heart went out to him. All night, I heard this man screaming and yelling in pain. It was something I will never forget.

The next morning, I woke up and it was silent. I didn't hear any screams. I called one of the nurses over and said, "I don't hear any screams; is he doing better?"

She replied, "No, he didn't make it." Right then was when I realized it could always be a whole lot worse! I told myself I would not complain about my situation anymore. Yes, I still dealt with the pain of being paralyzed at age seventeen, but I put things into perspective and I was thankful I was here and given a second chance at life, when that man did not . His life was over and my new life had just begun.

It's amazing what happens when you put things into perspective. No matter where you are in life or what is going on, you become more grateful for what you do have and focus less on what you don't have or your problems.

I had a newfound peace in my heart and so what if I was in a wheelchair? I was alive and I was thankful for it. There is a whole lot of life in front of me and I would get the most out of it!

If you are in a painful place in your life and feel like it is time to move forward, then here is what I want you to do. First, you have to ask yourself, "Am I the only person in the world who is going through this same problem?" I'll bet the answer is no. If I'm right, then the second thing I want you to ask yourself is, "Are any of them worse off than me?" I'll bet the answer is yes. Once you have come to this realization, the third thing I want you to do is to write down the positive things you *do* have in life. I'll bet you'll come up with a lot. The last thing is to remind yourself that you are here and pain does not last forever. Once you start putting these things into perspective, you will find the same peace in your heart I found in mine. Plus, you will now have the ability to move forward and that pain will no longer stop you. Trust me; I know.

"Embrace The Life You Have"

Fundamental Principle #3:

Accept there are certain things in life we cannot change. Forget about the pain from the past and move forward into your future.

Two thousand years ago, there was a Roman philosopher named Epictetus. He is one of my favorite philosophers. In his book, *The Art of Living*, one of the first messages he gives is, "there are certain things in life we have control over and there are certain things we don't have control over." The things we *do* have control over are our thoughts, our emotions, and how we respond in different situations. The things we *don't* have control over are the way people think or feel about us, things that happen to us, and outside circumstances. Often we try to control those things and quite frankly, that is impossible. I would sometimes worry myself sick thinking about the things I had no control over. Why? Did it resolve anything? No! Did it change the outcome? No! Did it change the way people thought or felt about me? You guessed it; no! I finally came to the realization that if I can't control it, I'm not going to worry about it. I have to tell you, once I did that, I felt a lot better. I focused on the things I did have control over: my own emotions, my hopes and dreams, and how I would react in different situations. When you accept this and start practicing it on a daily basis, you will experience less stress and worry with more inner peace and joy. To simplify it: life is ten percent what happens to you and ninety percent how you respond to it.

For years after my accident, I did not want to accept I would be in a wheelchair for the rest of my life. I constantly thought about how my life was before my accident. How active I was. How I would go surfing or Hydro sliding behind my boat. How much I loved working out and practicing martial arts. How much I loved riding my bike. How much fun I had dancing, not that I was that great at it, but I still had fun doing it. I simply missed how nice it was to be able to walk up to somebody and give him or her a hug. I was stuck in my past and was unable to move into my future. I had not yet accepted the one thing in my life I could not change.

It wasn't until I was about twenty-four when all of that changed for me. I decided living like this would not get me anywhere. I needed to do something different, so I turned to God. I prayed a lot and developed a relationship with Him. I needed to find strength and acceptance that I didn't have and He graciously gave it to me. It's amazing what the Lord will do for us if we simply ask. No longer was I fixated on my past and what I used to be able to do. I accepted I was in a chair now. I might not always be, but for right now, I am so I'm going to make the best of it. So what if I'm sitting? There was still a lot of things that I can do.

Shortly after that was when I took my first vacation after my accident. I went on a cruise with my father and a friend. I had an amazing time. While on the cruise, people told me that they admired that, despite my disability, I was still out and living life. That felt good. It inspired and motivated me to do more. So that is exactly what I did.

It was only three months until I went on my next cruise and now, since my accident, I have gone on a total of thirty-five cruises, traveled to over thirty different countries on six continents, and have taken a trip around the world. Not once have I ever looked back and wished I could have done it any other way. I am so thankful I have God in my life and He continues to give me strength and the desire to move forward and never look back.

Now I ask you to turn to God and ask Him to help you accept the things you cannot change and trust He will give you the strength you need to move forward into your future. Don't let life control your feelings. You are in control of your feelings, so do it now and watch your life change in amazing ways.

"Today Is A Great Day"

Fundamental Principle #4:

Instead of going through life with a defeated mentality, wake up every morning excited and declare today is a great day.

It is important to acknowledge that our thoughts, whether they are positive or negative, will have a direct effect on our day and ultimately—our lives. What we see in our mind and speak with our mouths is typically what we will experience in life. How many times have you woken up in the morning on the wrong side of the bed and it felt like from then on, your day continued downhill? Before you have even left the house, you already claimed it would be a bad day. Why do you do this to yourself? Do you own a crystal ball and can predict a bad day? If so, I would like to borrow it so I can check the stock market in the future. Since I'm sure you probably don't have a crystal ball, and you don't know how your day will go, don't claim it will be bad. Claim it is a great day! Have positive expectations.

In January 2009, my mother was diagnosed with leukemia. Her doctor said she had between six and twelve months to live. Hearing that news was the most devastating thing I had ever heard in my life. My mother, however, never let it get her down. She immediately went into the mindset of, "let's not waste any time and get busy with my treatment." Seeing her have that kind of attitude was extremely inspiring and made me proud to have a mother so positive and strong. The whole family rallied around her with positive words and encouragement. She immediately started her chemo and radiation treatments. During her treatments, she remained positive and always said, "This cancer is not going to beat me!"

Her treatment went on for the next six months and when all was said and done, her cancer had gone into remission. When we shouted, "Hallelujah!" and "Praise the Lord, thank you Jesus," you could have heard it a mile away.

Now, not only did her cancer go into remission, but also when she went back in September for a checkup, her doctor said, "Looking at your blood right now, if I didn't know any better I would swear it was your daughter's." It is amazing what prayer and the power of a positive mind can do. Because my mother held on to this attitude and would always claim victory over this cancer, we were blessed to have her in our lives a lot longer than the doctors ever thought.

Back in 1988, when I was in the hospital recovering from my accident, three weeks prior to being discharged, my father had a stroke. Now talk about having your hands full! I was in one hospital paralyzed from the neck down and my father was in another hospital paralyzed on one side. You would've thought my mother would go bananas, and yet she was a rock. My mother, sister, and other family and friends shuffled back and forth from hospital to hospital to visit us both. It almost became comical.

To make things even more interesting, my father and I got discharged from the hospitals on the same day. I was in a wheelchair and my father had a walker. Throughout my life, I have never seen my father let anything get him down or any obstacle get in his way that he did not overcome. Having to use a walker after his stroke was no different. For a few days, I saw my father struggle as he tried to get around, but I always heard him say, "I'm not using this thing for long!" Even though the doctors said that he would most likely have to use a walker for the rest of his life, not for one moment did he ever accept that.

Two weeks after we were discharged from the hospital, I saw my father get up from the kitchen table with his walker in front of him. He grabbed it, tossed it to the ground, and shouted, "I'm not going to use that crap anymore!" For a couple weeks, you would see my father walk with a limp, but not one time did he go back to that walker. In fact, after about three months, there was barely any sign he had had a stroke at all. Watching my father make that declaration, throw his walker to the ground, and overcome his obstacle was one of the most profound and inspiring moments of my life. After that, I made my own declaration that I will never let this chair stop me from achieving my goals in life and it never has, all thanks to the lessons taught to me by the two most amazing people I know: my mom and dad.

Here's what I want you to do (and what my parents would tell you also): only claim things that are positive. Declare it today—and right now—that you are made for greatness and you expect to see greatness in your life. In fact, say it out loud right now. Did you do it? Good! Now start moving forward in life, declaring every morning, "Today is a great day!"

"Don't Let Anyone Steal Your Joy"

Fundamental Principle #5:

D on't let anyone steal your joy or have control over your emotions.

One of the only things we truly have control over in our lives are our emotions; yet, so often we give that control to others. How many times have you driven down the highway and all of a sudden, somebody cuts you off? Now you are angry, honking the horn and yelling at somebody who can't even hear you and more than likely didn't realize they cut you off. Yet, you have let this person get under your skin and probably negatively affect the rest of your day. You have now let that person steal your joy and have control over your emotions.

For a long time in my life, I would let people get under my skin and allow anger to take over. Nothing good ever came from this. In fact, it would usually end badly. We have all heard the expression, "misery loves company." Even though we have heard the expression and we know the meaning, we still fall prey to those who are miserable. Again, what you have done is allow somebody to steal your joy and have control over your emotions.

Like I said earlier, I used to have a problem with anger. I would harbor resentment and even hatred toward somebody who had wronged me. There have been a couple of people in my life who I have done that with and sometimes it's lasted for years. What an incredible waste of time and energy that was, because I finally realized is my anger and resentment toward that person didn't do anything to *them*. They weren't affected. In fact, a lot of times they couldn't have cared less. That is when I decided I am not going to let people steal my joy or negatively affect my day. It is amazing how much your stress level will drop when you make that decision in life. I'm not saying after you make that decision, the next day you are going to be smiling from ear to ear and bulletproof from anyone's verbal attacks. It will take work on your part to develop the proper way of responding to negative people and negative situations.

I used the word *responding* instead of *reacting*. I did that on purpose. The word "react" often has a negative connotation. Think of a person in a hospital being treated for an illness. The doctors give that person some medicine to help, but instead they have a bad "reaction" to it. However, if the doctor gives that person medicine and they "respond" well to it, there is a much better outcome. We have all had those moments in life when we would "react" to something quickly. How many times did that work out well for you? If you are anything like me, the answer would be never. On the flipside, when you give your self the opportunity to "respond" to someone or something, typically the end result is much more positive and both parties turn out much happier.

I have met many people in life who love conflict and it appears like they are always looking to start an argument. I have also come to realize those people are not worth my time at all. I have already declared earlier that morning, "today is a great day," so there is no way I'm going to allow anyone to change that for me. Something that I also realized is when somebody is angry and looking for an argument, if you don't give it to him or her, you completely disarm him or her and remove any power they might have over you. I guarantee you will feel on top of the world when you do this.

It's funny how after I developed this principle and have applied it in my life when people would lash out at me or try to start an argument. I never let it happen. Some of my friends would say to me, "Man, I would've handled that totally different. I would've told them off and gotten right in their face. I would've been pissed off!" I would always ask them the same question. "So did that fix anything? Do you feel any better now that you did that? Now you're angry also."

The point I am trying to make with all of this is, quite simply, you are in control of your emotions and you can decide whether you want to "react" or "respond." So if you are ready to put this principle into effect in your life, I guarantee the life you see around you and the people you will see around you are going to be vastly different from what you are used to and you are going to love it! The people in your life who used to push your buttons and had some power over your emotions will start to fade into the distance. They will realize you have taken control over your emotions and how you respond in every situation. So the next time you feel like somebody is trying to steal your joy, remind yourself that you are in control and you have all the power over your emotions.

"Eliminate Can't And But"

Fundamental Principle #6:

Eliminate the words "can't" and "but." All those words do is allow you to come up with excuses.

It is amazing how powerful a word can be. Growing up, I am sure we all learned the same saying, "sticks and stones may break my bones, but words can never harm me." This is true; the words that people say to you should never harm you. However, some of the most damaging words we hear in our lives are the ones we say to ourselves. In my opinion, the most harmful words that we use are "can't" and "but." It will either stop us dead in our tracks or give us an excuse why we can't do something or why something positive won't happen. For example, "I can't possibly overcome this obstacle in my life because it is too overwhelming or I would have been able to have done it, but…"

There is a famous quote by Henry Ford, "Whether you think you can or you think you can't, you are right." I absolutely love this quote because it is simple and true. It appears to me sometimes people would almost rather use the word "can't" instead of "can," so no effort needs to be put into it and there is no disappointment if they fail. This is a case of either laziness and or the lack of belief in their abilities and the lack of faith the Lord will help them through this tough time. Say, "I can," believe in yourself, and have faith the Lord can and will always be there to help you. Do not ever question it or doubt yourself and especially, the power of faith!

By using the word "can" as much as possible when facing a new challenge, you are conditioning your mind and setting yourself up for success. A perfect example of this is what my beautiful fiancée did when she decided to go to college. When she made this decision, she chose not to tell anyone because she didn't want anyone to have the opportunity to say she can't. She was a twenty-three-year-old single mother with a full-time job. She would always say to herself, "I can do this." Even after she was there for a while, there were still those who said she couldn't. Thankfully, she never listened to people saying that word and two years later, she got her degree in business administration. Now she could've done what many people are guilty of and said, "I want to go to college, but I have a full-time job and a four-year-old at home and I am a single mother. There is no way I will be able to do it." Thankfully, she did not do that. She believed in herself, said "I can," and she did it. I am proud of her.

The word "can" is empowering; it tells you that you have the desire and ability to do something. Remember the story of the little engine that could? He kept saying, "I think I can, I think I can, I think I can." I want you to take it one step further and say, "I know I can, I know I can, I know I can!" Do this and succeed.

Now that you understand the importance and power of the word "can," you must make sure when using it, you do not follow it up by putting in the word, "but." I see people do this all the time and I used to be guilty of it as well. I would say things like, "I know I can do this, but because of this or that, I won't be able to." Using that little word, I allowed myself to come up with an excuse as to why I can't or won't be able to accomplish my goal. The word "but" is just as poisonous as the word "can't." Erase both of those words from your vocabulary.

The next time you are getting ready to do something, I want you to do it without hesitation. Do not question yourself or your ability to do it. Believe in yourself and say, "I can." Ignore any time you hear the words, "you can't," or, "you might have been able to do that, but what about this or that?"

"Follow Your Passion"

Fundamental Principle #7:

Follow your passion in life and you will always find success.

How many times in your life have you done something not because you wanted to, but because you were told to or you felt you had to? When you did it, did you give it your all? Did you put your heart and soul into it and even if you did, when you were done, was it something that filled your soul? This is something I have experienced from childhood all the way through adulthood.

46

I remember being a child and, didn't exactly get the best grades, at least not in the subjects that I had no interest. However, when it came to science and math, the two subjects I loved, I did exceptionally well. It boiled down to that was what I was passionate about and because of that, I was successful in it.

The same can be said when it comes to the career path that we choose in life. How many times have you heard somebody say or even heard yourself say, "I don't like my job but it pays the bills"? Unfortunately a lot of people fall into this category. If you are doing something in life you are not passionate about, it is hard to get excited about it and consider yourself successful.

I want to make sure we are on the same page when it comes to what it means to be successful. A lot of times, people equate success with making a lot of money. Sure, that is one way of thinking of success. However, if it is a job that makes you miserable, regardless of the money, can you consider it success? I know a lot of people who have a job where they make good money, yet it makes them miserable and have given it up to follow their dreams and their passion. Even though it meant taking a pay cut, they still did it. They found success in doing what they love. Isn't that what we all want—to do something we are passionate about and love to do? I guarantee you if you follow your passion, you will find success in many different forms.

In 2002, I decided to start my own nursing agency. I had no formal training in business. I had no work experience. To be honest with you, when I started the business, I had no idea what I was doing. However, the one thing I did have going for me was that for the past fourteen years, I had caregivers twenty-four hours a day, seven days a week. Also, for the last ten of those years, I was the one who was responsible for finding my own caregivers, conducting their interviews, doing their schedules, doing their payroll, and when necessary, firing them. I did this for myself because I realized early on I did not care for the way a lot of different nursing agencies were run. So after I had done this for myself for quite some time, I realized I had a pretty good knack for it, plus a much deeper understanding since I lived it all the time. So when I started my company, even though I had no idea what I was doing, it was something I was passionate about and I knew I would be able to succeed.

Because this was something I was passionate about, it almost felt effortless to do. Even though it took up a lot of my time, it never felt like that because I loved what I was doing. I learned a lot in a short period of time and before long, my company had gone from the dining room of my house to three offices with a little over three hundred caregivers. God had truly blessed me. It was a wonderful feeling knowing I was able to create something that provided so many jobs and also made a significant difference in people's lives. Don't get me wrong; the financial aspect of it was nice. However, when I would hear from a mother how much of a positive impact one of our caregivers made on her child, that was absolutely priceless. Because of moments like that and thankfully there were quite a few of them, I considered what I had accomplished to be rewarding and successful. I will always be thankful to the Lord for allowing me the opportunity to follow one of my passions in life.

So if you are in a place in life right now where you are doing something that is making you miserable and is not filling your soul and there is something else in life that you are passionate about, I encourage you to do it. If you have a dream, follow it. I have had people say to me, "What I want to do is already being done," and a lot of times, that stops them dead in their tracks. I would make a point to say to them, "So what? Why not use this as an opportunity to do it better than them?" We all have different gifts and talents and it is important to recognize them and use them the best of your abilities. Follow your dreams. Do what you are passionate about. Believe in yourself. You will find it will feel almost effortless because you are using the gifts and talents God gave you.

Now I want you to write down what it is that you are passionate about. Do not get overwhelmed by thinking there are a million things that must be done. Simply put down the first three things that are necessary in order to put it into action. Take it step by step. Once you have taken that first step, it is amazing how you will see God open doors for you and you will see success right around the corner.

"Be Thankful"

Fundamental Principle #8:

B e thankful for what you have and don't complain about what you don't have.

It feels like ever since we were children, we have been conditioned to always want something and to always want more of it or at least something else to go along with it. What makes it even worse is we would associate our happiness with whether we got it or not. This is sad. I remember as a kid going to the mall during Christmastime and waiting in line so I could sit on Santa Clause's lap and give him a list of all the things I wanted for Christmas. Well,

Christmas morning would roll around, and I was fortunate and blessed that my parents always went above and beyond for my sister and me. There were definitely more toys to play with than I knew what to do with. However, it still did not stop me from finding that one toy I did not receive and somehow now focusing on not having it, instead of being thankful for and appreciating all the other things I did receive. Talk about a spoiled brat.

All of this changed in a dramatic way. I want to add this took place when I was only six years old. My parents loved to travel, especially outside of the United States. They always brought my sister and me. It was their philosophy that there was a lot for us to learn that would not be taught in the classroom. This was never truer than when we visited Haiti.

For those of you who have never been to Haiti, it is an absolutely gorgeous island and the people are extremely friendly. Unfortunately, it is also a poor country. There's a level of poverty you do not see in the United States. It would leave you in shock and awe to see the reality of how so many people live outside of the United States.

Getting back now to our visit in Haiti. One afternoon, after lunch at a nice restaurant, we walked outside to get into our cab and small children swarmed the cab, begging for money. Several of them even stuck their hands inside the window. This is when I saw something that has forever changed my life and a memory I will never forget. A young boy, who was probably my same age, put his hands in the window and I noticed his hands and fingers were so badly burned, the skin in between his fingers had melted together, making it impossible for him to spread his fingers apart.

I immediately turned toward my mother and asked, "Why are his hands like that"?

She sadly replied, "A lot of times the parents will maim or disfigure their children so people will feel more sorry for them and give them more money."

No pun intended, but this was something that will forever be burned into my brain. Ever since that moment, I always tried to be thankful for whatever I had, no matter how big or how small. No matter where you go, you will always find somebody who has much less and would do almost anything to be where you are and to have what you have in life.

My father always taught me it is important to thank the Lord for all He shares with us and to recognize and be thankful for the things many people cannot be thankful for. I always tell people, when it comes to giving thanks and praise to the Lord, think about like when you were a child and you would receive something from a parent. When the parent gave you something and you failed to show or give thanks, do you think you would get anything else? Probably not. The same thing holds true with our Lord. He is generous and loves to give. However, if you do not show Him thanks and give Him praise, the chances of you receiving more from Him becomes slim.

When you are truly thankful for what you have in life, you are able to enjoy it to the absolute fullest. Although, if you constantly say, "I will be happier once I get this," or, "I will be happier once I get that," chances are you are never going to find true happiness because there will always be something else you want. This is a terrible way to live because you end up finding yourself on a treadmill of, "I want more and I need more!"

Here is your assignment: write a list of all the things you have and are thankful for. You will come to the realization that you are truly blessed and end up having more than you once thought. Not to mention, it will show you, you have much more than the majority of the people living around the world. So now get off that treadmill of, "I want, I want, I want," and show thanks for all you do have and get ready to see the Lord bring more and more into your life.

"Blessing Others Brings Blessings"

Fundamental Principle #9:

Find opportunities in life where you can help others and you will be amazed at what you see come back to you.

I have always said the way we become blessed is by blessing others. It feels like these days, everybody has the "me me me" mentality, when it should be "others others others." I cannot tell you how many times I have heard, "What have you done for me lately? What am I going to get out of this? How is this going to benefit me?" When did our society become so self-absorbed that we focus on ourselves instead of others?

My father's parents immigrated to the United States from Germany in 1910. They lived in Oklahoma City and opened a small grocery store shortly afterward. My father has told me stories about how my grandfather went above and beyond for his customers. Especially during the Great Depression when money was tight for everybody. Many times, his customers could not afford all of their groceries and he would ask them to pay what they could and he would make up the difference. He knew it was more important to help those who were in need. My father would tell me how amazing it was to see when these same people had the opportunity, they would go above and beyond for my grandfather and help him and his family in any way they could.

My father also told me stories about how he and his father would make wine in the cellar during prohibition. I asked my father, "How much wine would you guys make?"

He said about seventy gallons.

I said, "Oh my gosh, what would you guys do with all of that wine?"

He told me they would only keep about ten gallons and gave the rest to friends and neighbors. I told him it sounded to me like they were a couple of wine shiners. We had a good laugh about it. The point my father tried to make was it is more important to give than to receive. My father learned a valuable trait from his parents and he always carried it out through his entire life. I also experienced throughout my life—and so did my father—how amazing it was to see how people gravitated toward my father and always went above and beyond for him because of his kind heart and generosity. I am blessed and thankful to say this is a quality that has been passed down from generation to generation.

If this was not a quality passed down in your family, don't worry; it can be picked up easily. One of the easiest ways to start doing this is by simply smiling at others, especially complete strangers. Something I love to do on a daily basis is what I call "PET." It stands for Positive Energy Transfer. When I'm out and about, perhaps in a grocery store, I smile from ear to ear, say "Hello, how are you doing today?" and, "Have an awesome day" to every stranger. Maybe I look like the Joker and act like a Wal-Mart greeter, and some people may find it odd, but I assure you the reactions are extremely positive. We never know what is going on in another person's life at that moment, but more times than not, when they see a smile and hear kind words from a total stranger, it can turn their day and life around in an instant.

In fact, there was one day I was in a grocery store when I rolled past a woman who looked particularly distraught. I smiled at her and said, "Have a blessed day!"

She lifted her head, smiled, and she said, "Thank you; I will!"

I rolled on and went down another aisle and all of a sudden, she ran in front of me and said, "I just want you to know how much I appreciate what you did for me."

I said, "All I did was smile and say, 'Have a blessed day.'"

While grinning from ear to ear, she said, "And that is all it took to make my day!"

It was wonderful to know, by me doing something so simple, it changed the course of her day. For the rest of the day, I was on cloud nine and it felt like everything fit right into place for me. Because this is something I do daily, I can thankfully say I feel like this most of the time and it because of my kindness and generosity, others are more than willing to go above and beyond for me.

I want you to feel like this also. Wake up each morning knowing people will go above and beyond for you because they see how happy, joyful, and giving you are. Look for an opportunity to perform a random act of kindness. We are recognized and remembered for the little things we do in life. So the next time you start to think, "What is this going to do for me?" Say to yourself, "What is this going to do for others?" and you will find your blessings rolling in.

"A Calm Mind Equals Less Stress"

‿

Fundamental Principle #10:

A calm mind is a rational mind; an angry mind is a confused mind.

It is proven when you are calm and relaxed, you give yourself the ability to think clearly. On the flipside, when you are angry or upset, you are basically stupid. How many good decisions have you ever made when you are yelling and screaming? Probably none. So why do we yell and scream? Does it truly solve any problem or does it make things worse? I know in my own life, I have been in many arguments and I don't think at the conclusion of any of them did anyone ever say, "Okay, problem solved." A psychologist told me a long time ago that the moment people start yelling at each other, their ability to rationalize is over. No one wins. Unfortunately, it took me a long time before that sank in. Only when I made a commitment to God to let go of anger and be a better person did I start to apply this in my life. I came to realize anger is a waste of energy, emotion, and time. After I did this, I was much happier and so were the people around me. Of course this change did not happen overnight, but over time, and being conscious of my emotions and how I would react to things, it became easier and easier. Now, it is difficult if not almost impossible to get me truly angry. There is simply no point in it. People are sometimes amazed at how I am able to stay calm, even in a situation that would typically anger someone. When I am calm, my thoughts are clear, I am able to be rational and think logically. My emotions do not get in the way.

I've also found when somebody is angry and yelling at you, if they do not get it in return, it puts out the fire rather than fan the flames. I am willing to bet there have been times in your life when you have been in an argument and not only did you not get anything resolved, but things probably got worse. Then some time goes by, you calm down, and you are able to talk about things rationally. I am also willing to bet things got better.

If we are aware of this pattern, why do we repeat it? I am not saying everyone does this, but there are people out there who have anger as a natural instinct. I have also seen these same people have a difficult time trying to get their point across without upsetting somebody in the process and it usually never works.

Let's get on to something a little more positive. Let's talk about the benefits of being calm. Stress, deadlines, and surprises can get to us mentally and emotionally. Figuring out how to stay calm will, for obvious reasons, make your life a lot more enjoyable. We all know stress kills. It has been linked to heart problems, depression, and even posttraumatic stress disorder. To achieve a truly calm mind, I suggest you first try to detach yourself from the situation. If you cannot remove yourself physically from the situation, then mentally remove yourself from it or from the person creating it.

Second, let your emotions take a break. One of the biggest problems we have in life is we tend to think and react according to how we feel. Do not respond with a knee-jerk reaction. Take three deep breaths, let go of the emotions, and you will find things becoming a lot clearer and you will be able to focus on the solution.

Finally, this is my favorite: meditation, prayer, and visualization. I talk more extensively on this matter in another principle but I do want to touch on it briefly because I find it to be helpful when attaining a truly calm mind. Learning how to do this and practicing it regularly is a great way to reduce stress, anxiety, and find that calm mind, body, and soul. Now I am not suggesting if you are in a stressful situation, you run out of the room to go meditate, but what you should do in a situation like that is remind yourself of that calm relaxing feeling you experience when you meditate. Put these things together and you'll start to experience life in a new way. Life will become easier, more enjoyable, less stressful, and people will gravitate toward you and all you had to do was be calm.

"Being Positive"

Fundamental Principle #11:

P ositive thoughts bring positive results.
 We have all been asked this question at some point in in our life: are you a glass half-empty or a glass half-full kind of person? I like to answer that question by saying I am a glass overflowing kind of person. Even though this is a simple and not scientific question, I believe it tells a lot about a person and what they expect from life. I feel those who view the glass as half-empty expect more negative things to occur and live by Murphy's Law which is, anything that can go wrong will go

wrong. In my opinion, that is a horrible way of looking at life. You are basically waiting around for something bad to happen so you can say, "See I told you so."

I have met a lot of people in my life who think this way and say those same words. I would ask them afterward, "Are you happy you were right?"

They would say, "No, but I knew it would happen."

Of course it would happen—that is what they expected. Now I am not here to tell you that as long as you have positive thoughts, nothing bad will ever happen to you, but I am here to tell you to get rid of the negative thinking. It does you no good. Change your mindset from a glass half-empty and negative thinking to your glass being half-full and even overflowing. Take a more positive approach toward life and you will give yourself the opportunity for more positive things to happen. Research has shown positive thinkers are healthier, less stressed, and overall have a greater well being. Whenever you are faced with a stressful situation, positive thinking will help you cope with it more effectively. I read a study that shows when a positive thinker encounters something disappointing in life, they are more likely to focus on the things they can do to resolve the situation as opposed to dwelling on the frustration of something they cannot change. Thinking positively will help you to devise a plan of action to give yourself more options, and in turn, be more successful. Whereas thinking negatively will stop you dead in your tracks because now you have assumed the worst and feel like there is nothing you can do. I believe people get what they expect. A positive thinker expects a better outcome than somebody who thinks negatively, and typically you get what you expect.

A perfect example of a negative thinker is somebody I know; let's call her Sally. Sally always told me how bad things are, how bad people are, she never gets any breaks, and nothing ever works in her favor. The list went on and on. The sad thing is she was right; nothing did go her way. It appeared like her life was filled with doom and gloom until one day when she told me there was an eviction notice on her door. Her landlord wanted her out. Unfortunately there had been a history of arguments between them and the landlord had enough. While talking to Sally, she told me all the bad things that had taken place between her and the landlord. There was nothing that could be done to change her mind. However, I was able to convince her to take a more positive approach to the situation. I told her the first thing she needed to do is get rid of the negative thinking and focus on a more positive outcome to the situation. After she did that, I instructed her to call the landlord and with a considerable amount of humility, apologize for her previous transgressions.

At first she said, "That's not going to change anything."

I said, "Not with that attitude it won't, but if you try it my way, I guarantee you—you will see something positive come from it."

It took some convincing, but she finally did it. Along with the phone call I also advised her to bring her a card showing how sincere she was. To make a long story short, she never got evicted and now she and her landlord get along beautifully. Using positive thinking gave Sally options on how she could resolve her situation and ultimately have a much better outcome.

Another aspect to positive thinking I want to make clear is you must also believe it is your reality. I have met many people who have said, "I am being optimistic, but I am also being realistic." First of all, we know we should not use the word "but," because all that does is negate your first thought and opens the door for negativity.

Secondly, if your reality is negativity, then you are not being optimistic. So you are contradicting yourself by saying you are optimistic, which is being positive and then stating that your reality is the opposite, which is being negative. You cannot have both and still have a positive outcome. Choose positive thinking. Make it your reality. Believe in a positive outcome. Visualize it in your mind. You will find life less stressful, more enjoyable, you will live longer, and I am positive you will be much happier.

"Making A Few Adjustments"

Fundamental Principle #12:

You will always be able to achieve your goals in life. You may need to make a few adjustments along the way.

In 1988, when I was in the hospital after my accident, I would have a weekly meeting with the doctors and therapists. During every one of those meetings, the doctors always told me everything I couldn't do. They said, "You have broken your neck and you can't walk. You will never walk again and you will never do this and you can't do that."

Week after week, I heard the same thing over and over again. After hearing this for a few weeks, it became a downer. In fact, one of the days before the meeting, I said to my father, "Do I have to go to the meeting today? I don't like them."

He looked at me and said, "Don't worry about it, son. I will take care of it." He rubbed my head and walked out the door.

When he came back. I anxiously asked him, "What did they say? What did they say?"

He said, "The doctors had nothing new to say. Now you have heard them tell you all the things you can't do; now I want you to hear me and focus on the things you can do. You can use your mind, which means your possibilities are limitless. You can see, so you can appreciate all the beauty around you and you can hear, so you can listen to beautiful music." The more he talked, the better I felt.

He went on to say, "You will always be able to achieve your goals in life. You might have to make a few adjustments along the way."

I am so thankful he spoke those words to me because he was absolutely right! When I was younger, one of my favorite movies was "Top Gun." I watched Tom Cruise fly around in that fighter jet doing flips and loops. I said, "One of these days that is going to be me!" Well of course after I broke my neck, that didn't happen. Do you know how hard it is to find a fighter jet with a wheelchair lift on it? It is impossible! However, I never let that stop me. In 2007, I was able to fly in a fighter jet piloted by a Top Gun instructor. The whole time, I told the pilot to fly faster, flip upside down, and do more barrel rolls. The pilot said, "You are an animal!"

I said, "This is a dream come true for me, so I am going to get everything out of it I can. Now fly faster!"

He appreciated my enthusiasm and flew that plane as if we were in a real dogfight. That was an incredible experience and one that I will always be thankful for. I didn't stop there. I went skydiving eighteen times. Of course I was always strapped to somebody else. I went scuba diving dozens of times, which entails somebody dragging me through the water. I was fortunate enough to even be able to dive with over forty sharks in Nassau. I've traveled all around the world. I have never let this chair stop me from doing anything. I have never said, "I can't."

I owe this "can-do" attitude to my father. Growing up, I saw my father face severe adversities many times and not one time did I see him waver. Not one time did I see him get down in the dumps. I will never forget the day when he told my mother, sister, and me he had cancer. We were all devastated, but he looked like he come from the dentist and found out he had a cavity. A few hours later, I went by my parents' house to check on my father. Can you believe he was outside washing the car? I said, "Dad, what are you doing out here washing the car? You just found out you have cancer!"

He said, "Cancer's not going to wash the car. I still have to do it."

That was in 2006 and now, in 2015, there is no sign of that cancer. Praise Jesus! To give you another example of his perseverance and can-do attitude, recently he had some issues with circulation in his right leg. Keep in mind— he is ninety years old. Because of the lack of circulation in his leg, the doctor told him that he had to get two toes amputated.

When we were in the doctor's office, I asked my father, "What do you think about losing two of your toes?"

He said, "Fine by me. I wasn't too attached to them in the first place."

I can thankfully say this man is my father, my mentor, and my best friend. Now I want to share with you some of the same words my father shared with me in that hospital room so many years ago. I'm sure some of you have heard some negative things in life that have probably kept you from achieving your goals. Guess what? They were all lies! Here's the truth: you were made for greatness. You can overcome any obstacle and you will be able to achieve your goals in life. You may need to make a few adjustments along the way.

"Peaks And Valleys"

Fundamental Principle #13:

You ou will always have peaks and valleys in life. However, what you do in the valley will dictate your next peak in life.

Life will always be filled with ups and downs. Both are necessary because if you didn't have any downs, how would you grow and how would you truly appreciate the ups in life? If every day was a sunny day and there was no rain, would you truly appreciate those sunny days? Probably not. It is amazing to see when people are doing well and on a peak in life, they are happy, joyful, filled with faith, and give thanks and praise to the Lord. However, if something bad happens, if there is disappointment or some kind of a setback, people are unhappy, they lose their joy, their faith begins to fade, and they start asking God, "Why have you forsaken me?" Have you ever thought that maybe the reason you are in that valley is necessary to prepare you for your next great peak? It is stated in the Bible that all things work for the greater good for those who have faith and love the Lord. It should be enough to point that out and be done with it. However, for some people it is not that simple.

There been many peaks and valleys in my life and in the beginning, I will admit, I sometimes viewed them as setbacks. I can thankfully now say that I viewed them as setups. Several years after my accident, I was fortunate to receive a fairly large settlement. This money was supposed to take care of me and pay for my medical expenses for the rest of my life. It was a huge blessing having this.

Everything was great until 1998 when I invested some money with the wrong person and was conned out of a half a million dollars in real estate that never existed. On top of that, the financial advisors who managed the remainder of my portfolio lost almost all of it through bad investments in 2001. I sued them and in August 2002, we went to court. Unfortunately or fortunately, depending upon how you want to look at it, I lost. I now faced an uncertain future. I did not have the money to pay for around-the-clock nursing, let alone normal living expenses. People thought I was doomed. Yet, the next month, I opened my own nursing agency. I had no knowledge or experience in opening or running a business. However, I knew caregivers since I had been having around-the-clock care since 1998. I also knew I'd better make sure this business worked; otherwise I would be up a creek without a paddle.

The biggest thing I had going for me though was my faith that God had something much bigger in store for me. I can't say I had many people rooting for me, but it didn't matter because I knew I had God rooting for me and that is all I needed. I dove in headfirst with passion, commitment, and a strong belief in being successful.

This company was founded in my dining room and within a few years, and by the grace of God, I was able to build it to three offices with over 300 employees. When I look back now, upon that day in court in August 2002, I thank the Lord that I lost! God had something much bigger in store for me. I could've done what most would do and what a lot of people thought would happen to me—roll over and be defeated. If I had done that you probably wouldn't be reading this book right now. I was in a deep valley and because I stayed in faith, knew God had something bigger planned for me, and I was passionate about what I did, I ascended to a higher peak.

This is not the only valley that I went through that took me to a higher peak in life. Anytime I go through a valley in life, I hit the "rewind" button and remind myself how great God is and, the truth behind the verse, "all things work for the greater good for those who have faith and love the Lord!"

The next time you find yourself in your valley, stay in faith, know God has something bigger in store for you. Figure out what you can do to make this valley work for you and not against you. Do not let one disappointment or setback stop you from moving forward. Understand, accept, and be thankful a rainy day is necessary in order for you to be able to appreciate and be thankful for the sunny days ahead.

"Finding Your Success"

Fundamental Principle #14:

Having more stuff is not necessarily a sign of success.

Years ago I saw a documentary what makes people happy and how they define success. Almost everyone they interviewed had the same response to, "What would make you happy and consider yourself successful?"

"Making lots of money," was the response I heard over and over again. Making money is important because we all have bills to pay; however, if you feel money is the only thing that will bring true happiness, you are going down the wrong path in life.

They were also asked, "What would you do with all of that money?"

Again the responses were similar: "Buy lots of stuff. A huge house, lots of cars, expensive clothes and jewelry." They wanted material objects. The problem with having this mindset is it is never enough. You are going to find yourself on what I like to call a "materialistic treadmill." There is a hole in your life that can only be satisfied by purchasing something. You buy something, the novelty wears off, and hole comes back and you find yourself at the store again, looking for something else to purchase. This process repeats itself over and over again and now you are on the materialistic treadmill finding it hard to get off.

I will admit there was a time in my life when I found myself rolling on that same treadmill. The whole time I thought, "if I buy this or if I buy that, I will be happy and life is good." Boy, was I wrong. At the end of the day, all I had to show for it was a huge credit card bill, a bunch of stuff I didn't care about, and looking for something to make me happy. This stuff did nothing for me and it definitely didn't do anything for anyone else. What a waste of money!

While attending church one Sunday morning, thankfully all of that changed for me. It was close to Christmastime and our church has a program where you can adopt a family for Christmas. The premise of the program was to assist some families who struggled financially and give them a Christmas they wouldn't have otherwise. This was an amazing experience. The first family I adopted was a single mother of three. I called her up to introduce myself and let her know I was with the church. It was touching to hear how thankful she was for the church and for my phone call. When I asked her what I could do to help make this Christmas more special, I was touched by her humble and simple request. Initially I expected to hear a long list of toys for kids; however, that was not the case at all. She shared with me she didn't want anything for herself and her only request was to have new shoes for her children. To say that touched my heart is an understatement. I immediately thought about all the times I would go shopping for stuff I did not need. It put things into perspective for me. I let her know I would absolutely do that for her children and then some. I also asked her what she needed or wanted.

She instantly replied with, "Oh please; nothing for me. I am grateful for what you can do for my children."

I said, "When you were a kid and went to the mall and sat on Santa's lap, would you have a hard time asking him for something?"

She said no.

I said, "Think of being that child again and let me know what it is that you need or want."

It took a little coaxing, but I was finally able to get it out of her. After I got off the phone with her, I called up the church and told them I wanted to adopt a few more families. I realized quickly true happiness does not come from the accumulation of stuff for yourself. It comes from the accumulation of stuff you can do for others. There is nothing you can buy or own that will give you the same kind of happiness and joy you receive when you do something for others and make a difference in their lives. Now I'm not telling you from here on out you can't buy anything for yourself, because we all need things, and an occasional treat here and there is not bad. What I am saying is there comes a time when enough is enough. The definition of success is the accomplishment of an aim or purpose. If your purpose in life is to simply put a smile on somebody's face each and every day, and you do it, then you are successful. If your purpose is to raise your children the best you can and you do it, then you are successful. Whatever it is that you aim to do in life, if you do it to the best of your ability, you are successful. Base your success on the things you do, not on the things you have.

"You Are Limitless"

Fundamental Principle #15:

The only limitations you have in life are the ones you put on yourself.

After my accident and finding myself confined to a wheelchair, paralyzed from the neck down, I was told I would be limited with what I would be able to do in life. This is the last thing an active seventeen-year-old wanted to hear. Nonetheless, this is what I was told by a lot of people, except my father. My father told me while I was still in the hospital, "You have your mind and with that, your possibilities are limitless!"

I have to admit—in the beginning, I had a hard time wrapping this around my mind. I knew what he meant by it; I didn't know how I would implement that in my life. I knew this for sure: I am would not sit in this chair and watch the rest of my life pass me by.

I was blessed from the beginning with family and friends who were supportive and never treated me any different. That was a huge help. There were still a lot of things I wanted to do in life and I would not let this chair stop me from accomplishing them. It all goes back to what my father shared with me in the hospital room when he said, "You will always be able to achieve your goals in life; you might need to make a few adjustments along the way." I started to think about things in a different perspective. I figured I could do anything anybody else can do; I only have to do it a little differently.

It started with little things like going out with my friends. Sometimes the parties would be on the third floor at an apartment building and there was no elevator. I didn't let that stop me; nor did it stop my friends. It was always a good feeling when we climbed all those stairs and saw the look on people's faces as they stared in amazement that nothing would stop me. I was blessed with friends who helped me overcome any obstacle. Even though it probably doesn't sound like an earth-shattering accomplishment—going to a party—for me it was the first step in realizing there is no obstacle I could not overcome!

Not only did doing things like that give me a great deal of confidence, but I also noticed I inspired others by overcoming these obstacles, which was a great feeling. When I saw some of the things that I did inspired others, that inspired and motivated me to continue to push forward and do more. I eventually got to the point where I went skydiving and scuba diving. I was even able to fly in a fighter jet piloted by a top gun instructor. Now that was a dream come true. The look on the faces of the people who ran the fighter jet company was priceless when they saw me rolling up to the plane. It took about six people to get me in that fighter jet but it was all worth it. Now if you are wondering whether or not I got sick during the flight while we were doing all the flips and loops the answer is no, thankfully.

As I look back on my life after my accident, I am blessed to say not only did I not lose who I was, but I feel my disability has enhanced my life and I wouldn't change it for the world. So what's the point in all of this? I am not sharing these things in order to say, "Look at what I have done!" I am sharing these things to prove with or without a disability there will always be obstacles in life.

What's the point in all of this? How you handle obstacles makes all the difference in the world. There is no obstacle to large to overcome if it is something you truly desire. Never think to yourself, "I can't do this because I can't do with that person does." So what? Find a way you can do it and who knows—you might do it better. Never underestimate the power of the human spirit. Let your passions drive you in life. Have the mentality that there is nothing you can't overcome. It is amazing the strength the Lord will give you as long as you believe in Him and in yourself. I have seen too many people give up before they even tried. We have all heard the expression, "Push it to the limit." I want you to know there is no limit, and there is no limit to what you can do. Live every day to the fullest because you never know what tomorrow will bring or if it will come at all.

"Meditation And Prayer"

Fundamental Principle #16:

D aily meditation and prayer is a great way to find clarity and inspiration.

It's the end of the day and you had a hard day at work. You have run errands all day. You had to pick up the kids from school. Traffic was the worst. Your nerves are shot and you are wound up like a top. The best thing for you and those around you would be for you to be able to sit back and relax. Unfortunately, your thoughts of the day keep spinning around in your mind and you find it hard to do so. This was a problem that plagued me for years and

I needed to find something that would help. I could've popped open a beer or poured myself a drink, but that wouldn't give me the results I wanted. I knew there had to be a different way to find it.

That is when I came up with meditation and prayer. I would start off by using a breathing technique called the six-two-six. This is a technique that was developed by the CIA for their agents. Basically, you breathe in slowly through your nose for six seconds, hold it for two seconds, and breathe out slowly through your mouth for six seconds. Do this three times and you will be amazed at how it will relax you.

After that, I would clear my mind of any thoughts. At first, it was a bit of a challenge to simply clear my mind of any thoughts, but after practicing, it became easier and easier. I would concentrate more on my breathing and let my mind drift with the music. I would use different techniques such as visualizing myself walking down a flight of stairs counting backward with each step until I got to the bottom. Once I was there, I pictured myself in a place so relaxing and peaceful, I couldn't help but fall deeper into a relaxing trance. For me, it was sitting on the beach in the Dominican Republic as the waves crash against the shoreline. The sky was black which made the stars, the constellations, and the edge of the galaxy shine so brightly. I had found my place of zen. Once I found myself in this deep sense of relaxation, and self-hypnosis, I replayed my day and focus on all the positive things. I thought of every smile, every laugh. If there was an event that took place that didn't go the way I wanted, I would change my memory of it to one that had a more positive outcome. Slowly but surely, I would smile from ear to ear. My body immediately felt lighter, as if whatever negative weight was on me was gone.

Now I was in the right frame of mind to pray and truly connect with the Lord. I thanked Him for all the wonderful things He has and continues to do in my life. I thought of the times I found myself in a valley and He always brought me out and placed me on my next peak in life.

It is a comforting feeling when you remind yourself of all the blessings you have received from the Lord because you know if He did it before, He will do it again. I thought of everything positive in my life, from my past to my present, and even into my future. The more you focus on the positive, the better you feel and the better you feel, the more positive you are.

Sometimes I would take my meditation and prayer one step further and add in visualization. I would take an upcoming event or situation and visualize it in a way that was positive and pleasing to my soul. I did visualization for things I desired or wanted to take place in my life. I focused on these things and repeated them when I would do my meditation and prayer.

If I were to tell you how many of my visions came to fruition, it would probably shock you. I have to admit, at first it shocked me, but I quickly realized how powerful prayer, a positive outlook, and the human mind truly is.

The other benefit of meditation and prayer is finding true inspiration. I have found when I am able to have a calm mind, body, and soul, when I feel engulfed with positive energy, and my heart is open to God's Word, I am flooded with inspiration. By the time I'm done with my meditation and prayer, I feel rejuvenated, happy, inspired, and motivated to achieve my goals and desires. By then, I've completely forgotten about the things that took place that bothered me. Now you're probably wondering how often you should do this. The answer is every day. As far as time, I do it anywhere between thirty minutes to sometimes over an hour. I recommend starting out for at least fifteen minutes. After doing this for a while, you will find it easier to fall into a deep trance. You will also quickly realize how good it makes you feel and before you know it, you will find yourself doing it for thirty minutes, an hour, and maybe even longer. This is a valuable tool if you want to live a happier, more joyful, and successful life. I know it will make you feel better and you will see positive results sooner than you think. This principle is extremely important and valuable. You will be glad you chose to do it.

"Go With The Flow"

Fundamental Principle #17:

Life is like being in a canoe on a river. If you are fighting against the stream, the scenery never changes, you go nowhere and it is exhausting. If you go with the flow, the scenery is constantly changing, beautiful, and effortless.

I know you are probably looking at this principle and thinking it is a long one. Well, you are right; it is a mouthful; however, I feel the analogy is perfect for describing how many people go through life. In this principle you will use some aspects from other principles in order to make this work best for you. It all starts out with: there are certain things in life we have control over and there are certain things we do not. When you try to control the things in life you have no control over, it is like paddling against that stream. You end up going nowhere and the only outcome is frustration.

It is important to recognize the things that happen in life that you have no control over. Once you have identified these things, you have to accept them for what they are. This doesn't mean you say, "I have no control over it so I will give up." Instead, focus on things you do have control over. Remember: you have control over how you interpret things, how you respond to what happens in life, and ultimately what you do to try to resolve these issues.

Once you do this, it will feel like you have turned that canoe around because instead of fighting against the stream, you flow with it. You have now eliminated the wasted energy and frustration and you now have the clarity and energy necessary to come up with more positive options.

This touches on the benefits that come with having a positive attitude, which leads to positive thoughts, and eventually positive results. Having positive options is much like the scenery changing as you flow down the river. You are no longer stuck in one place. You have now been able to make a big change in your life. You are going with the flow, you are no longer wasting energy, and you have eliminated a considerable amount of frustration and stress.

Your next step now is to implement the positive options you have been able to come up with. Believing in yourself in visualizing a positive outcome benefits you greatly. It is an absolute must that you exercise your faith and know God will always bring you out of your valley in place you high upon your next peak. You have to be passionate about it and give it your all. I want to remind you these things do not happen overnight; it takes time, patience, and the willingness and desire to make a change. It is amazing to see that after doing this for a while, life becomes effortless. Keep in mind, as you travel down the river of life, there will be times when the waters get rough and things will change. Don't panic though, because you know what you need to do in those situations; you need to make a few adjustments along the way. Remember, there are no limits to what you can do. Be creative. Remember the old adage: if at first you don't succeed, try again. Always be able to find a way to achieve your goals in life. You might have to do it differently than you once thought; you might have to do it differently than others, but who cares. At least you will achieve that goal and who knows—you might inspire somebody along the way. We only get one crack at life, so don't waste it by fighting against it; enjoy it by simply going with the flow.

"Seeing a Positive Life"

Fundamental Principle #18:

Only speak into existence the things you want to see in life.

Something profound I learned in life from my father is in the forty-five years I have been alive, I have never once heard my father speak negatively about his life or the lives of those around him. He has always and still has a positive outlook on life even at the age of ninety. Every morning he starts his day on a positive note, looking forward to a great day and expecting to see positive things throughout the day. The wonderful thing is to see that is primarily what he gets every day. Sure, I have seen him go through some serious adversities in life and yes, there would be times when negativity would occur; however, it would never last long and he didn't focus on them.

I started to realize at an early age that the things you talk about and focus on are primarily what you see in life. It is a simple concept and sounds so easy to do, so why are we not doing it all the time? I have found a lot of people will say, "it sounds too good to be true," or, "It can't be that easy." Believe it or not, it is. We sometimes forget how powerful words can be and it's not only the words we speak, it is the thought and emotion that goes along with it that's powerful.

Here is a simple example and one we are all familiar with: how many times have you have said to yourself, "I know I'm going to get sick; I can just tell I'm going to be sick," and before long, you are sick. I am quite sure you have because I have done this myself many times. Instead of saying, "I know I'm going to be sick," say the opposite and claim and speak into existence you feel great and you know you are not going to get sick. Chances are, you won't. I know this probably sounds silly to you and you might even be thinking that doesn't work. I want you to know you couldn't be more wrong. The things we say in life, whether they are positive or negative, are ultimately what will occur—a self-fulfilling prophecy.

This is a big reason why I start every morning by saying, "Today is a great day. I will see smiles and laughter everywhere I go. People will go above and beyond for me because they see how happy, joyful, and grateful I am. I am thankful for all the blessings I received from the Lord." When you start your day with this mentality and claim it, you have now spoken it into existence. It doesn't stop there. I want for you to believe in your heart, mind, body, and soul that is exactly how your day will go.

As you are getting ready to leave the house to go to work or to school you need to continue to say positive things such as, "I know there won't be any traffic and I will be able to get to where I need to be on time. Work or school is going to be awesome today." It is a much better feeling when you use positive thoughts and positive words when thinking about things you need to do.

Secondly, you have a better picture in your mind for how your day will begin to unfold.

The third thing is expectation. It is important you follow all of this up with positive expectations. Remember, we always find what it is we are looking for. Always expect and look for those things you talk about and picture. You'll be amazed at the shift in the world around you.

Much like the other principles, this takes time, practice, and faith in the process and of course, faith that the Lord will help you to see this. Let's face it—we all want to love a better and more positive life, otherwise I wouldn't have written this book and you probably wouldn't be reading. That is why I will always continue to say it is important to be optimistic and to make that optimism your reality. Like I have stated before, there are a lot of people who will say, "I am being optimistic, but I am also being realistic." If your reality is not positive, then you are not being optimistic. It's as simple as that. Whether you believe in this principle or not, you will find out life will unfold in the exact same way you talk about and what you expect to see.

"Kind Words Open Doors"

Fundamental Principle #19:

Kind words are the best way to see doors open wide.

Often I find myself on the phone with somebody from technical support trying to troubleshoot a problem with my cable or Internet (or anything electronic) that I don't understand. The one common factor when I talk with all of these different people is the majority of the time I am able to get them smiling and laughing. Not only does it make me feel good, but it especially feels good when they say, "I needed this today. You don't realize the day I have had. This is the first time I have laughed all day." Now I am not doing these things with the intention that if I make them smile and laugh, they're going to go above and beyond for me. I am doing these things because I love to make people laugh and if I am given the opportunity to make a positive change in someone's life, even if it is for a brief moment, I want to do it.

Remember: how do we become blessed? By blessing others. The wonderful and blessed thing that occurs after doing this for others is how often people are more than willing to go above and beyond for me. I always let them know how grateful I am for what they do for me and I always ask them if there is a manager or supervisor I can speak with so I can let them know how pleasant they were and how they went above and beyond for me. I believe it is important to do this because it always feels like people are quick to complain and slow to compliment. I would have friends or caregivers in the room when I am on the phone talking with some of these people and they would be so amazed at what the people on the other end of the phone would do for me. They say, "Man, how did you do that? They are never that nice to me and they definitely wouldn't have done all that stuff for me."

I asked them, "When are on the phone with these people, are you personable and having fun with them, trying to make them smile and laugh?"

Typically they answered with, "No; why would I?"

I responded, "Then why would you expect them to go above and beyond for you if you won't start by going above and beyond for them?"

Here's another way of looking at it: put yourself on the receiving end of this scenario. If a friend or relative or even a complete stranger comes to you needing your assistance and they are nasty, demanding, wanting you to drop everything you are doing, immediately are you going to jump up with a smile on your face feeling joyful and happy and say, "Sure thing! What can I do to help you out?" I am willing to bet chances are you would respond in a different way and I wouldn't blame you.

There is an old saying that says you attract more flies with honey than you do with vinegar. Another way of looking at it is if you are kind and have a positive attitude, chances are that is exactly what you are going to attract in your life: kindness and positivity. I have applied this principle in my life for quite some time now and I truly feel it is a large piece to the puzzle of living a happier, more joyful, and successful life. I have said other principles might not necessarily happen overnight, but they will happen. The cool thing about this principle, however, is you will be able to see positive results almost instantaneously. It is because every time you speak or interact with somebody, you have the opportunity to be kind, use kind words, and make people feel good.

I know we have all heard and know the saying, "treat others the way you would like them to treat you." I don't know about you, but I have heard this since I was a small child. I will admit, it might've taken a while before it truly stuck in my mind and I applied it in my life, but what a difference it has made. I am constantly blessed by others who would go above and beyond for me and I have seen doors open wide right before my eyes. It is also nice to know I am able to leave a positive and lasting impression in other people's lives.

Once you apply this principle in your life, you will begin to see amazing things happen in your life and in the lives around you. Plus the feeling you will have while you do this and the positive results that it has is amazing and kind of addictive. In fact, you are going to start looking for more and more opportunities where you can be kind to others, not necessarily because you want something from them, but because you realize how great it feels to make others feel good.

"Know Better, Do Better"

≈

Fundamental Principle #20;

Know better, do better.

Ever since my accident in 1988, I have required around-the-clock nursing. I can't even begin to tell you how many different people and from all walks of life have helped me throughout the years. I could probably write a book on the caregivers I have had in my life. Thankfully, I can say I have been blessed with more good ones than not-so-good ones and I have got some great stories to go along with each and every one of them.

I must say there is one who stands out in the crowd; her name is Lena, a sixty-three-year-old Indian woman who was born and raised in Guyana. She is four foot nine and weighs all of about ninety pounds. When she first started working for me in the year 2000, she didn't know she was my caregiver. She thought she was the housekeeper for the first six months. When she told me this, I of course had to giggle and then I asked her, "So when it came to giving me a shower, did you think I was thorough with the housekeeping?"

She said in her tiny voice, "I never know boy; I never know."

I knew Lena was a keeper about a month after she started working for me. I was in bed one evening with terrible shoulder and neck pain. I asked her if she could rub my neck. She started to and then I asked her if she could dig her thumb into my neck. She said, "No boy I cannot do that."

I said, "Please, Lena. It is the only way it will feel any better."

Again she replied quickly, "No I will not!"

I said one last time very sincerely, "Please Lena, stick your thumb right into my neck."

She said, "Okay fine," then proceeded to crawl onto the bed with her tongue out.

Shocked, I said, "What are you doing?!"

She said, "You said to use my tongue."

I said, "No Lena; your thumb not your tongue. Your thumb!"

I thought to myself, anyone who is willing to stick their tongue on someone's neck in order to make them feel better is definitely a keeper. I can thankfully say Lena is still with me to this day and has provided me with so many great stories along the way.

When Lena grew up in Guyana, she unfortunately had to drop out of school at an early age, because in her culture they had arranged marriages and the girls were usually married off at a young age. Because of this, Lena missed out on a lot of formal education. That doesn't matter though because what Lena might be lacking in book smarts, she more than makes up for with what she shares with her heart and how enlightened she truly is. She is by far one of the most thoughtful, kindhearted, and giving person I know. The way she looks at life and how she deals with her peaks and valleys is truly inspiring. I have learned a lot from her throughout the years and the one thing that has stuck with me the most is when she first said to me, "Know better, do better." It is amazing how impactful and powerful those four simple words are. There are many things we learn in life such as what is right and what is wrong. Yet, even after knowing what is the right thing to do, we still often do the wrong thing. Why? It doesn't help us, nor does it help anyone else.

I find myself in situations when I con-template how I should respond at that par-ticular moment. I often catch myself hearing those words in my mind, "Know better, do better." That would instantly make my decision on what to do simple— do the right thing. Because I do know better, in fact, I am quite sure you know better as well. The more that I would apply this principle in my life, the happier I became and so did those around me. I would find if I was in the middle of a conflict with someone, regardless of whether they did the right thing or not, as long as I knew I did the right thing, there was always a = more positive outcome. Isn't that what we all want, a positive outcome? Sometimes doing what is better might involve swallowing your pride and being humble, but I guarantee you, it will pay off in the end.

I also noticed when you decide to do better you encourage and inspire others to do better. You lead others to have a more joyful life as opposed to following in the opposite direction. The first step you need to take in order to apply this principle in your life is to think

about the first fundamental principle, which
is you must make a conscious decision you
want change in your life. By doing this, you
are stating you want to do better. The second
step is to make sure you do not react in certain
situations without giving yourself the opportunity to think of a better way to respond. The
third step is easy; do it. Of course, with anything, it is something you must practice daily
and be committed to it. You'll find life is less
stressful, more enjoyable, and those around
you will appreciate the things you do. The
next time you find yourself in a situation wondering which direction to go, remember little
Lena saying, "Know better, do better."

"Putting It All Together"

Fundamental Principle #21:

Listen, learn, apply, and share.
Here we are at fundamental principle twenty-one. In many respects, this is one of the most important principles of all of them. The reason I am saying this is because if you haven't listened, you haven't learned anything. If you haven't learned anything, there is nothing to apply, and of course now you have nothing to share. Fortunately, I doubt this is the case.

This principle does not apply to only what I have shared with you in this book; it applies to everything in life. All throughout life we are blessed with moments where we have the opportunity to learn. There will never come a time in our life when we know everything. I believe it is important to learn something new every day. However, in order for us to learn anything, we must first listen. Listen to our teachers, listen to our parents, listen to our children, listen to our boss, listen to our employees, listen to our peers, and listen to life. When you give yourself the chance to listen, you will be amazed at how much is out there to learn.

Make sure what you are listening to and want to learn is something that is positive and will enrich your life and the lives around you. Unfortunately, I have seen where some people would listen to the wrong thing and in turn, learn something detrimental to them and those around them. I am confident if you have listened, learned, and applied the pre-vious twenty fundamental principles, you will know how to avoid the wrong thing and filter out anything negative.

If you have listened and learned, what good is it if you don't apply it? I'm going to give you what you might think is a weird analogy, but ask yourself, why is it most diets never work. You listened to that infomercial at three in the morning, you bought all the stuff, it finally came in the mail, and you read and learned everything you were supposed to in order to have that body you have always desired. Months later and instead of having that ripped body, you find yourself on the couch ripping into another bag of chips. Why didn't it work? You know everything you are supposed to do; however, you didn't follow it up with the next big step: applying it. Having knowledge and not applying it is like drowning in the ocean and not grabbing the life preserver next to you.

Maybe the analogy of drowning and using the life preserver is more fitting because as the life preserver can save your life, applying what you have learned with these 21 fundamental principles can save your life as well, but in a different way. It will save you from having a stressful life. It will save you from being stuck in a rut. It will save you from unnecessary pain. It will help to encourage you to follow and live your dreams. It will help you overcome any obstacle in your way. It will help you make a positive difference in people's lives. You will realize there are no limits to what you can do. You will realize life is better than you ever thought possible. You will realize you have strengths, talents, and gifts you did not know were there. You'll see people going above and beyond for you. You will see doors open wide for you. You will see opportunities you haven't seen before. You will experience blessings on a monumental scale.

Now that you have listened, learned, and applied these twenty-one fundamental principles in your life, you now have the great opportunity to share them. I believe there is no point in having anything in life, whether it is something material or having knowledge, if you do not share it with others. It is our duty in life to share what we have with others. No matter how big or how small it is, you can always find someone who can benefit from what you have to offer. Remember, we are all going through this life together. Some of us take it step by step, while others are simply roll along.

Lightning Source UK Ltd.
Milton Keynes UK
UKOW02f0844280217
295492UK00001B/5/P

9 781498 468534